Dear Parents and Teachers

I am Clarissa Della. I have dedicated my life for making the world a better place. M
changes in the society and I always believed that our thoughts and words have th

I always think how different the world would be if all the children out there were taught the words of love, compassion, and humanity! The idea to write such a book emerged from that very thought.
Inside this book, you will find an easy and delightful way to empower your kids to become the best versions
 of themselves. This book will make your children a better human being.

You may use this book as a tool for conversation and to create meaningful connections with your kids.
The concept of this book is a great source for both children and adults.

With this book, I want to nurture the heart, imagination,
and potential of kids all around the world.
To all the parents and teachers out there –

Thank you for sharing this
 alphabet with your children.

Regards,

Clarissa Della

This book belongs to

_____

A is for Admiration

Admiration is to praise others for their good deeds.
I always admire my friends for their helping mentality.

B is for Bold

Bold is having the courage to do the right things in life. If I am protesting against any injustice, I am being bold.

C is for Caring

A caring person is the one who thinks of others in their sufferings. I am caring when I help a wounded bird.

D is for Devotion

Devotion is the love and loyalty to a person or activity.
I should have devotion for my family.

E is for Endearing

Endearing is to arouse feelings of love and affection among others. I become endearing when I help a senior citizen cross the road.

F is for Friendliness

Friendliness is to be good-natured towards others.
My friendliness makes others comfortable to talk to me.

G is for Grateful

Grateful means to be thankful to others.
I am being grateful if I appreciate what others did for me.

H is for Honesty

**Honesty is being truthful all the time.
I am showing honesty if I admit what I did.**

I is for Ideal

Ideal means to be the most suitable.
I am being an ideal person if I am abiding
by the law of the society.

J is for Justice

Justice is to ensure fair judgment for everyone.
I can do justice to everyone if I am being kind to them.

K is for Kindness

Kindness is taking care of others. I am showing kindness if I am helping my granny to go upstairs.

L is for Loyalty

Loyalty means to be faithful and devoted.
Having loyalty to my family is the best thing I can do.

M is for Merciful

Merciful is being considerable to others. I am merciful to others and help them understand their mistakes.

N is for Noble

**Noble is having high moral values.
If I am not harming the nature, I am being noble.**

O is for Obedient

Obedient is listening to advices from the elders.
I am being obedient when I listen to my teachers.

P is for Patience

Patience is being calm in tough times. I always hold my patience if I forget something in the exam hall.

Q is for Quietness

Quietness is the freedom from noise and disturbance.

I always enjoy the quietness of the nature.

R is for Responsible

Responsible means to keep your promises.
I am being responsible if I am taking care of my dog.

S is for Sociable

**Sociable is being friendly to everyone.
If I am friendly with my class, I am being sociable.**

T is for Tolerance

**Tolerance is the acceptance of different beliefs.
If I am accepting others opinions, I am showing tolerance.**

U is for Unselfish

Unselfish is to put the good of others above my own interest. If my classmate has lost her pencil and I am giving her my pencil, I am being unselfish.

V is for Vigort

**Vigor is to show energy and enthusiasm for a task.
I am showing vigor if I am helping my mom with her chores.**

W is for Wisdom

Wisdom is having deep knowledge on something. My wisdom helps me overcome any problems in life.

X is for Xenial

**Xenial is to be hospitable to strangers.
If I am helping a stranger with an address, I am being xenial.**

Y is for Youthful

Youthful is to be lively and active.
I feel youthful when I play with my friends.

Z is for Zeal

**Zeal is having great energy to achieve something.
I have zeal for being the best student in my class.**

Showing Kindness

Kindness helps us to take care of those who are in distress.
You will feel happy and joyful if you be kind to others.
Can you think of an instance when you showed kindness
to a person?
What are some other ways to be kind?
How can you be kind to yourself?

Examples of Kindness

Helping an elderly person to
cross the street.

Take care of a wounded dog.

Offering food to homeless people.

Showing Honesty

Honesty is to be truthful all the time. Truth is the most beautiful thing in this world and by being truthful one can make the world even brighter.

What are the ways to show honesty?

What can honesty bring you in return?

Who was being honest with you the other day?

Examples of Showing Honesty

Admitting your fault after you have done something wrong.

Telling the truth to your parents.

Return the pencil you found to its owner.

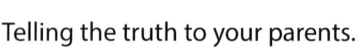

Being Unselfish

Unselfishness helps a person to become a better human being.
When you be unselfish, you will feel compassion for others.
How unselfish are you?
What unselfishness has gained for you?
How can you become more unselfish towards others?

Examples of Being Unselfish

Offering your seat to an elderly person on a train.

Sharing your food with others in your class.

Let your friends play with your toys.

Being Caring

If everybody becomes caring to each other, the world could be better place to live in. Care is one of the biggest virtues you can show to others.

How can you be caring to others?

Has anyone took care of you the last time you got sick?

How caring do you think the nurses are in the hospital?

Examples of Being Caring

Visit your friends if they are absent in school for a long time.

Help the school janitor in keeping the compound clean.

Help your granny to walk down the stairs.

Thank you for sharing this book with your children to empower themselves with humanity, kindness and compassion.

Printed in Great Britain
by Amazon

78464081R00020